HIDDEN HUMAN
COMPUTERS

THE BLACK WOMEN
OF NASA

BY SUE BRADFORD EDWARDS
AND DUCHESS HARRIS, JD, PHD

CONTENT CONSULTANT
DUCHESS HARRIS
PROFESSOR AND CHAIR
AMERICAN STUDIES DEPARTMENT
MACALESTER COLLEGE

Essential Library

An Imprint of Abdo Publishing | abdopublishing.com

ABDOPUBLISHING.COM

Published by Abdo Publishing, a division of ABDO, PO Box 398166, Minneapolis, Minnesota 55439. Copyright © 2017 by Abdo Consulting Group, Inc. International copyrights reserved in all countries. No part of this book may be reproduced in any form without written permission from the publisher. Essential Library™ is a trademark and logo of Abdo Publishing.

Printed in the United States of America, North Mankato, Minnesota
112016
012017

THIS BOOK CONTAINS RECYCLED MATERIALS

Cover Photo: NASA
Interior Photos: NASA, 6–7, 39, 46, 48, 51, 52–53, 60–61, 79, 82–83, 88; Duchess Harris, 15, 59; Beverly Golemba/NASA, 13, 44, 56, 67, 72; Dennis di Cicco/Science Source, 16–17; Lock & Whitfield/Wellcome Library, London, 21; Felt & Tarrant Mfg Co/Library of Congress, 23; Wilberforce University, 26–27; Frances Benjamin Johnston Collection/Library of Congress, 30; Library of Congress, 34; Hulton Archive/Getty Images, 36–37; Thomas J. O'Halloran/U.S. News & World Report Magazine Photograph Collection/Library of Congress, 62–63; NASA Technical Reports Server, 68; AP Images, 74–75; Tom Tschida/NASA, 90–91; David C. Bowman/NASA, 95, 97

Editor: Rebecca Rowell
Series Designer: Maggie Villaume

PUBLISHER'S CATALOGING-IN-PUBLICATION DATA

Names: Edwards, Sue Bradford, author. | Harris, Duchess, author.
Title: Hidden human computers: the black women of NASA / by Sue
     Bradford Edwards and Duchess Harris.
Other titles: The black women of NASA
Description: Minneapolis, MN : Abdo Publishing, 2017. | Series: Hidden heroes |
     Includes bibliographical references and index.
Identifiers: LCCN 2016910293 | ISBN 9781680783872 (lib. bdg.) |
     ISBN 9781680797404 (ebook)
Subjects: LCSH: Aerospace engineers--Juvenile literature. | African American
     astronauts--Juvenile literature. | Women astronauts--Juvenile literature.
Classification: DDC 629.45--dc23
LC record available at http://lccn.loc.gov/2016910293

CONTENTS

INTRODUCTION

Black girls and femmes love math. We love the intricacy and geometry of our braids, cornrows, curls, and coils. We like playing with building blocks, calculating how to make structures that will stay up and look good. Not too long ago, ancestors such as Harriet Tubman studied the location of the Drinking Gourd constellation—the Big Dipper—to lead black slaves to freedom. Math and astronomy have always been part of our story.

Far too often, American society has not known how to make room for this interest and ability in math as black girls and femmes grow into adulthood. Stories are told about whether we are smart enough, whether math is for us, whether we need to focus on homemaking or clothing, as if we have to choose between being fashion mavens and mathematicians. For this reason, many have turned away from any kind of love for mathematics.

I was lucky to be encouraged at an early age and allowed to play with my blocks until I was ten, at which point I began a journey that would lead me to the heart of the universe. As a particle physicist who uses math to describe the universe when it was less than a second old, math is my everything. This dance of loving numbers and representations of numbers has helped me make a life for myself and taken me around the world, from my birthplace in Los Angeles, California, to New York, Germany, South Korea, and Taiwan.

But I did not get here purely through love of mathematics. There were black women who came before me in the field of space science. They were part of a group of computers—human calculators who did computations before machines could do them. This was a job women were uniquely allowed to do in science, even though they were excluded elsewhere. A lot of this had to do with the fact that the job was hard. Doing the kind of calculations a modern machine does required periods of long, intense focus. It was considered beneath the dignity of smart men.

But without this work, there would be no successful human space missions. Our satellites would crash and go off course. Even though the work these black women computers did was devalued, it was essential to this scientific enterprise.

Their work was also hard in another way. As black women who lived in a segregated United States, they, like so many of us today, had to overcome the belief that by virtue of their gender, sex, and race, they were not qualified to participate in science. The women described in this book are proof that people like me are possible.

It is a joy to inherit the mantle of their great mission: a love of mathematics and a belief that all of us are entitled to love it. With this book, we hand the torch to the next generation of black girls and femmes—the mathematicians and astrophysicists of the future.

—Chanda Rosalyn Sojourner Prescod-Weinstein

Chanda Rosalyn Sojourner Prescod-Weinstein is one of fewer than 100 black American women to earn a PhD in physics. A former NASA Postdoctoral Program fellow, Dr. Prescod-Weinstein subsequently held a Martin Luther King Postdoctoral Fellowship in physics at MIT. As a researcher at the University of Washington, she studies where particles come from and worries about the dark matter problem.

CHAPTER ONE

NASA'S SECRET

Annie Easley and the other five women computers hurried through the building, eager to see the photograph that had been taken for an upcoming open house. The photograph of all six women at work was enlarged so visitors could get a view of what they did each day. As computers, they performed mathematical calculations for the engineers at the National Aeronautics and Space Administration (NASA) Lewis Research Center in Cleveland, Ohio. When the women saw the photo, one of the other computers turned to Easley and apologized. "Oh, Annie, they cut you out of the picture."[1]

The fact that something was cut from the photograph wasn't surprising. Photographers crop anything that looks out of place or might

Annie Easley played an important part at NASA as a computer, but the agency treated her as lesser because of her skin color.

DATE UNKNOWN

It is hard to say exactly when Annie Easley was cropped from the photograph of the Computer Services Division at the Lewis Research Center. Easley did not mention the exact date in the interview she gave NASA historians, but she started working at the lab in 1955, so the event must have taken place sometime after that.

"I didn't feel like I'm a minority . . . I'm out here to do a job and I knew I had the ability to do it, and that's where my focus was, on getting the job done. I was not intentionally trying to be a pioneer."[3]

—Annie Easley, NASA computer

steal the viewers' focus from the central image in the photo. This time, the photographer cropped out Easley, the only black woman working alongside five white women. Easley spoke to her supervisor, also a woman, about what had happened. "Oh, I don't blame you," she said. "I'd be upset, too."[2]

Although Easley had her supervisor's sympathy, nothing was done. At that time, there was no Office of Diversity and Equal Opportunity. Today, this office is responsible for ensuring NASA gives all employees the same opportunities. When Easley was cropped from the group photo, there were no laws that made this type of discrimination illegal, and there was no one to follow up on a complaint of this kind. Just like that, Easley was removed from view and hidden away.

Human Computers

Today's electronic computers process and save vast amounts of information. Scientists use these machines to make predictions about the weather and the spread of disease and to record the genetic makeup of a wide variety of plants and animals. The first computers were very different from those of today because they were human beings. These people did computations, completing complex calculations before there were calculators or other electronics to help get the job done.

In the 1700s, the first computers worked in astronomy. Both men and women ran numbers to solve problems for European astronomers, scientists who study the stars and planets. These computers helped the astronomers calculate the paths of planets and comets orbiting the sun. They estimated when these celestial bodies would complete an orbit and when each object would reach certain points in its orbit. It could take weeks or months for a computer to solve a problem, and it cost a lot of money to pay a computer to work so many hours.

Scientists could not always afford the services of these computers, but the military could. By the 1800s, computers were still calculating the movements of the stars, the planets, and the moon, but they were doing it to aid ship captains with navigation. Because this work

NAVIGATING BY THE STARS AND PLANETS

Ship captains relied on the stars and planets to navigate using a technique known as celestial navigation. They used the North Star most often. In the Northern Hemisphere, it is always to the north, hanging above the North Pole.

Navigators could also use the planets to navigate, but the position of other planets in relation to Earth changes. This is because every planet in the solar system orbits the sun, but each does so at different rates. Navigating by planets required complex mathematical tables constructed by astronomers and human computers.

was done through Great Britain's Royal Navy, all the computers were men. When human computing was used to create a navigational almanac in the United States, women again joined the ranks, crunching numbers and solving problems. Still, these women were white. Black women such as Easley did not work as computers for the National Advisory Committee for Aeronautics (NACA), which later became NASA, until World War II (1939–1945).

Swept under the Rug

Before World War II, job choices for educated black women were limited to nursing and teaching. Because of this, many women interested in math decided to teach it to others. It was not until World War II that NACA hired black female mathematicians, including Easley, Katherine Johnson, and Kathryn Peddrew. NASA continued to hire black women mathematicians in the 1950s and beyond. For example, Christine Darden joined the government agency in 1967.

Until recently, few people other than their families remembered the work these women did for NACA and NASA. Their accomplishments remained hidden from sight because they faced two layers of discrimination as both women and as blacks. Much like the many black women who worked for civil rights, these black computers were pushed into the background and forgotten.

"You can be anything you want to. It doesn't matter what you look like, what your size is, what your color is. You can be anything you want to, but you do have to work at it."[4]

—Annie Easley's mother to Annie Easley

Despite such discrimination, these black women graduated with degrees in mathematics at a time when many people thought the field was inappropriate for white women, let alone for black women. In the face of widespread prejudice and legalized discrimination, the black women who worked as NACA and NASA computers succeeded because other people inspired them. Easley's mother encouraged her to follow her dreams. Johnson's father was a math whiz. Darden fell in love with math when she was in high school and studied it throughout college, where a professor helped her find a job as a college research assistant in physics.

Thanks to the opportunities NASA provided, more than 400 women, both black and white, found something they were good at and wanted to do.[5] They did not listen when people said math was not for them and that no one like them had done these jobs before. They overcame many obstacles and stand as inspirations for today's mathematical girls.

The black women who worked as computers for NACA and then NASA, including Mary Jackson, *front row, right*, serve as role models for girls who like math and the sciences.

MIRIAM DANIEL MANN

Miriam Daniel Mann also worked as a human computer. She was born in Covington, Georgia, in 1907. Her father was a barber, and her mother was a teacher. Miriam graduated from Talladega College in Talladega, Alabama, with a degree in chemistry, but she studied mathematics as well, making it her minor. She returned to Georgia after graduating and married William S. Mann Jr. The couple moved to Hampton, Virginia, so he could be a professor at Hampton Institute. She began working at Virginia's Langley Research Center as a computer in 1943. She faced segregation there. Her daughter, Miriam Mann Harris, explained:

> She would relate stories about the "colored" sign on a table in the back of the cafeteria. She brought the first one home, but there was a replacement the next day. New signs went up on the bathroom door, "colored girls."[7]

Miriam Daniel Mann worked as a human computer until 1966, including when NACA became NASA. In addition to working in the wind tunnels, she worked on the craft John Glenn rode in when he became the first person to orbit Earth. And she was present when he came to show his appreciation for all the computers' work. Mann died in 1967.

Mann worked for more than 20 years at NASA as a computer, all while raising three children.

CHAPTER TWO
HUMAN COMPUTERS

Human computing began after Halley's comet was discovered in 1705. Astronomer and mathematician Edmund Halley attempted to calculate the comet's orbit around the sun. Although he never succeeded in finding a simple mathematical formula to describe the comet's path, he realized the gravitational pulls of the sun and the planets Saturn and Jupiter influenced the orbit. He believed another astronomer would succeed where he had failed. And he was right.

That astronomer was Alexis-Claude Clairaut. In 1758, he invited two friends, astronomer Joseph Jerome Lalande and astronomer and mathematician Nicole-Reine

Halley's comet shone brightly in California's night sky in February 1986.

Lepaute, a woman, to help. Working together, the three mapped the comet's orbit, adjusting the path as it would be influenced by the gravitational pull of the sun and the Earth. Lalande and Lepaute worked on one side of a table, then passed their work across the table to Clairaut. He reviewed it, looking for possible mistakes.

The three labored for five months to calculate the various dates the comet would reach certain points in its orbit. When they completed the calculations, Clairaut announced the comet would reach its perihelion on approximately April 15, 1758. Clairaut explained the most accurate prediction would be March 15 to May 15 because there were so many variables to consider. The comet was first sighted on December 25, 1757, by a German astronomer. It reached the perihelion on March 13.

Pure Science versus Number Crunching

Astronomers such as Clairaut, who worked with mathematics and employed human computers, were often criticized by others in their field. Although Halley's comet reached its perihelion only two days before the range Clairaut predicted, critics focused on the single date and complained about how badly he and his workers had miscalculated the date. French astronomer Jean Le Rond d'Alembert claimed Clairaut's work was not based in scientific inquiry. What Clairaut accomplished, according to d'Alembert, was rough and only approximate. By using human computers and running the various computations, d'Alembert said the work became laborious without being deep or meaningful.

Clairaut carefully checked Lalande and Lepaute's work for errors. Even a small error in such a complex calculation could seriously skew the results and make them useless. Because of this possibility, critics, including author Jonathan Swift, claimed mathematics and computing were too flawed to capture the nature of the universe.

Despite this criticism, scientists who could afford to pay someone else for the hours of labor required for mathematical calculations hired computers whenever possible. Letting a computer perform calculations freed the scientist to do other things. However, few scientists could afford to pay computers for weeks or months of labor.

Computers Go Military

While scientists continued to create theories that could be tested through observation, computers shifted their efforts to navigational astronomy. Fortunately, the military needed to know the movements of the planets and stars so ship captains could navigate the oceans, plotting their way from one land mass to another.

George Airy was England's astronomer royal from 1835 to 1881. He treated the human computers like soldiers. These young men, ages 13 to 20 years, were employed as part of the British Royal Navy. They worked long hours to test and calibrate the navy's chronometers, which are clocklike devices that help a captain determine his ship's longitude, or east-to-west position on Earth. His staff also processed a backlog of observations. The boy computers filled out worksheet after worksheet with computations. Because the supervisors were higher in social standing than the computers, they could get by with pushing them hard.

George Airy took his role as England's astronomer royal seriously, acting as a taskmaster to the young men and boys he managed.

Human Computers Reach the United States

In the mid-1800s in the United States, a computing group was formed to create the *Nautical Almanac*, a book describing the positions of the stars and other celestial bodies of use to ship captains. Instead of working together in offices, the American computers worked from their homes. Similar to the British computers, they did everything by hand. They wrote mathematical formulas on paper, looked up operations in tables, and calculated the results. Once they had compiled the information into an easy-to-read format, such as a table, the computers mailed their work to the director responsible for putting the almanac together.

In the mid- to late-1800s, mechanical calculating machines came into use. One popular machine was created by Frank Baldwin. The machine was powered by a crank on its side. William Seward Burroughs developed another machine, the Arithmometer. It was four feet (1 m) tall and stood on four legs. Dorr Felt also created a calculating machine. His was the Comptometer. It was the size of a cigar box or hardcover dictionary. It featured rows of buttons labeled 0 through 9. Although the human computers no longer had to do everything by hand, calculating machines were too expensive for individual

Comptometer

Our largest competitor claims that in one of its recent models — an infringing imitation of the Comptometer — it has an adding and calculating machine that is

"Just as Good as the Comptometer"

Its salesmen have been making this claim throughout the length and breadth of the land for over a year.

Of course, when pinned down close, they often admit that—"It is not quite so good as the Comptometer, but pretty near as good."

But don't you believe it.

The Comptometer is the only thing ever made that will stand that smashing of the rapid key-action to which a one-motion machine is subjected.

For years the usual comment has been, "The Comptometer cannot be improved upon.".

But what was seemingly impossible has been accomplished.

Add
Multipl
Divid
Subtra

New
Controlled-Key Duplex Comptome

Model E
Compels Correct Operation

Are you afraid of making a mistake due to fumbling a neighboring

You *can't* do it on the Controlled-Key Duplex Comptometer:— Because interfe guards at the side of each key-top prevent the operator, while touching one key, accidentally depressing a key in a column at either side of it.

Are you afraid of making a mistake due to a partial down-stroke of the key?

You *can't* do it on the Controlled-Key Duplex Comptometer:—Because if the operator give key a partial down-stroke, all the other columns of keys are automatically locked until the mista corrected by completing the downward stroke of the mis-operated key.

Are you afraid of making a mistake from not letting the key clear up?

You *can't* do it on the Controlled-Key Duplex Comptometer: Because on the up-stroke the ope cannot reverse the travel of the key until a full stroke has been made.

These three fundamental improvements mark a new era in adding and calculating machine construction. *They completely eliminate the possibility of error from a fumbled or misoperated key.*

The machine will not *allow* you to proceed until the is corrected.

computers to own. Because of this, they could no longer work from their homes and had to work in central offices.

In the two decades following the American Civil War (1861–1865), women moved into the field of computing. They filled vacancies that would normally have been filled by male workers if these young men had not died in the war. High schools were teaching their students business skills, and women who had taken these classes went to work in the central offices of various businesses. In 1875, one in 600 office workers was female.[3] By 1885, this number had increased to one in 50.[4] By the early 1900s, most of the computers were women. This shift occurred because companies could pay females less than males. In fact, the field

THE WOMEN COMPUTERS OF WORLD WAR I

The women who became computers during World War I (1914–1918) were from wealthy white families that could afford to send them to college. The first woman hired by the US Army in 1918 was Elizabeth Webb Wilson. She had a degree from George Washington University and had won the school's mathematics prize. She said her job at the US Army's Experimental Ballistics Office saved her from having to attend high society parties and other events in search of a husband. When men returned to work after the war, Webb and the other women computers lost their jobs. An insurance company hired Webb to use her mathematical talents to prepare actuary tables, which list the probability a person of a certain age and gender will die before their next birthday.

was so completely taken over by women that when mathematicians discussed the amount of effort or time needed to complete a job, they discussed it in terms of "girl-years" or "kilo-girls."[5]

With the onset of World War I (1914–1918), many women computers focused on military matters. They calculated trajectories, which are the paths artillery shells take, and atmospheric drag, which is the pull of air on the body of an aircraft (also called wind resistance). Many of these wartime computers worked at the military testing area known as the Aberdeen Proving Ground and for the National Advisory Committee for Aeronautics. During World War II, black women began filling these jobs. They calculated trajectories, drag, and more.

ABERDEEN PROVING GROUND

Founded in Maryland during World War I, Aberdeen Proving Ground is a test facility where experiments are performed to prove weapons of various kinds will function as planned. During World War I, the US Army used the site to test ammunition, big guns fired from train cars, and field artillery such as cannons. Women computers worked at the proving ground, producing the tables soldiers in the field used to aim their weapons, angling them based on their distance from the target. During World War II, mathematically inclined black women began working at the proving ground, testing guns, tanks, and other equipment.

CHAPTER THREE
EDUCATING BLACK AMERICA

Before the American Civil War, educating
slaves was illegal. Free blacks could go
to school if they could find a school. Few
"nonblack" colleges would admit black
students, and there were only three black
colleges in the United States. The first of these
schools was the African Institute in Cheyney,
Pennsylvania, which became the Institute
for Colored Youth (now called Cheyney
University). The school began in 1837 with
$10,000 from Richard Humphreys, a white
Quaker silversmith. He specified in his will
to establish a school for those of African
descent. Members of the Quaker religion often
worked against slavery, and this became the

Members of Delta Sigma Theta sorority at
Wilberforce University, the oldest private
historically black university in the United
States, 1922

first school in the United States where African Americans could receive a higher education. The faculty members were black.

The second school was Ashmun Institute, which was later renamed Lincoln University in honor of Abraham Lincoln. It was established in 1854 in Chester County, Pennsylvania. Although this was one of the earliest black schools, there were no black faculty members until 1932.

The last pre–Civil War school for blacks was Wilberforce University. Wilberforce was established in Wilberforce, Ohio, in 1856. It became a stop on the Underground Railroad. The school thrived until the Civil War. During the war, enrollment and financial support dropped off, and the school closed its doors in 1862. Someone purchased the school and reopened it the following year. After the war, additional schools opened to meet the need for black education.

Black Universities

In 1865, Congress established the US Bureau of Refugees, Freedmen, and Abandoned Lands, commonly called the Freedmen's Bureau. The bureau worked to help former slaves and poor whites in the South as they struggled to find jobs and support their families following the war. The Freedmen's Bureau provided food, medical assistance, and housing. It also established schools. Many of these schools were for African Americans.

Former slaves wanted the education they had been denied. They knew education would help them move forward as they organized black communities, entered new professions, and took part in government. They attended the new schools that came into being through the Freedmen's Bureau as well as those founded by religious groups and philanthropic organizations that worked to improve the lives of former slaves.

One of the new schools was Hampton Normal and Agricultural Institute, founded in Hampton, Virginia, in 1867. The institute is now called Hampton University. The money to create this school came from the American Missionary Society, which worked to create educational opportunities for blacks. The school helped students gain agricultural and

WHAT THEY TAUGHT

In addition to learning the skills needed to find and hold a job, the first Hampton students also studied etiquette and morality. Their studies in morality included the difference between right and wrong as well as temperance, or not drinking alcohol, and how to be respectful. These lessons in morality were included in their curriculum because General Samuel C. Armstrong, the director of the Freedmen's Bureau, believed immoral behavior was a problem among black people.

Students at Hampton in 1899 studied the Earth's rotation around the sun in a mathematical geography class.

mechanical skills. One of the first graduates was Booker T. Washington, a former slave who later became an author and speaker. He founded the Tuskegee Institute, a well-known and respected black university.

Black Communities

With these new schools, the number of blacks entering careers in science slowly rose, but most of the newly educated were men. Black women still had the lowest incomes, often doing farm work or domestic labor. Despite this, black women and men were being educated in larger numbers than ever before. Instead of studying science, black women studied for professions that were common in developing black communities, becoming teachers, medical professionals, and lawyers. Many black women who chose medical professions earned their degrees from the new black colleges, such as Meharry Medical College or Howard University. Others attended predominantly white colleges in the Northeast.

As many as 200 hundred black communities were established after the Civil War.[1] In these communities, black families could own land and their own businesses. Residents could also escape racism and prove they could govern themselves. Some of these towns were in former slave states, including Mound Bayou, Mississippi, and Shankleville and Kendleton, Texas. But most were in the West, where land was cheap.

GRAND CONTRABAND CAMP

During the American Civil War, the commander at Fort Monroe in Hampton, Virginia, was Brigadier General Benjamin Butler. A lawyer by profession, he was also an opponent of slavery. When slaves escaped to the fort, Butler decided that, because Confederate states considered slaves chattel, or property, his refusal to return escaped slaves to their Confederate masters made these former slaves "contraband of war."[2] Simply put, by considering them property, former slaves were goods the North could not give back to their enemies. Butler established the Grand Contraband Camp, a place where former slaves could live and not fear reenslavement from Confederate soldiers.

POST–CIVIL WAR BLACK COMMUNITIES TODAY

The communities established by freedmen after the Civil War were often rural. At the center of these communities were one-room schools and small churches. Little more is known about life in towns such as Hobson City, Alabama, or Rentiesville, Oklahoma, because few records survive. Other communities, such as Chapel Hill, North Carolina, are still thriving, but they have changed. Today, the younger descendants of former slaves are moving to other communities to live and work. Because this is possible, these communities no longer shelter black residents as they did in the past. Having new residents means not everyone is descended from a former slave, and the focus shifts away from a community's post-slavery history. Because of this, historians are working to preserve as much of the history as possible. When these towns look a lot like the surrounding communities, historians want young people today and tomorrow to remember why they were founded.

Many of the people who moved into black communities were skilled tradesmen. They had been trained as slaves. Because of this, these communities had blacksmiths and brick makers. The first buildings the settlers put up were usually a church and a school, and these became the center of the town. In order to live as free people, the residents needed to learn, and education was important in these black towns. Such communities had a strong need for teachers. Black women with degrees in education could find jobs at the new black schools.

These communities also needed other businesses and services. Blacks worked in their town banks and post offices. They provided their own health care, and black women earned the degrees to hold health care jobs. In 1864, Rebecca Lee Crumpler became the first African-American woman in the United States to earn a medical degree. In 1890, Ida Gray became the first black woman to earn a doctorate in dental science. Other women followed, providing the health care needed in their communities.

Black Science

As women entered various scientific fields, they often found work as teachers, passing their knowledge on to others. One of these women was Josephine Silone Yates. In 1879, she graduated from Rhode Island State Normal School with a science degree. She also took her teacher's examination and

REBECCA LEE CRUMPLER

Rebecca Lee Crumpler was a nurse before she attended the New England Female Medical College in Boston, Massachusetts. She graduated in 1864, making her the first black woman physician in the United States. Crumpler earned her degree 15 years after Elizabeth Blackwell became the first white female doctor in the United States. When the Civil War ended, Crumpler moved her practice from Boston to Richmond, Virginia, where she could provide health care for newly freed slaves.

"I early conceived a liking for, and sought every opportunity to relieve the sufferings of others."[3]

—Rebecca Lee Crumpler

Josephine Silone Yates was a successful student
and teacher.

earned the highest score the school had ever seen. Passing this exam made her the first African American certified to teach school in the state of Rhode Island, but she moved to Jefferson City, Missouri, in 1879. There, she took a job at Lincoln University, a black college. She taught chemistry, English literature, and elocution, or speech. Yates became the first woman to receive a full professorship at Lincoln and was appointed head of the Department of Natural Sciences in 1888. She was such a popular teacher that Booker T. Washington invited her to become the "lady-principal" at Alabama's Tuskegee Institute in the late 1880s.[1] She declined his offer and remained in Missouri, giving up teaching when she married in 1889 and started a family.

Another early black woman to study science and teach in her field was Beebe Lynk. In 1892, Lynk earned a degree from Lane College in Jackson, Tennessee. In 1901, she started studying pharmaceutical chemistry at the University of West Tennessee, learning to make medications. She graduated in 1903 with a doctoral degree and immediately took a job teaching at the university. Education remained the field of choice for many scientifically minded black women into the 1900s, particularly until World War II.

CHAPTER FOUR

FLIGHT AND FIGHT

In the early 1900s, as increasing numbers of African Americans attended college and studied science, they did so in a world that was changing fast. Much of this change, ranging from the completion of the Panama Canal in 1914 to Albert Einstein's development of the theory of relativity in 1915, had to do with technology and science. Although advances were being made in many scientific fields, US aircraft lagged behind both US automobiles and European aircraft. Many Americans considered the airplane a passing fad that was too dangerous to pursue, given the number of pilots who died in crashes.

Airships such as the German navy's L2, a dirigible, prompted the United States to form the National Advisory Committee for Aeronautics.

Americans realized how important aircraft were after World War I broke out in Europe. German dirigibles, large football-shaped balloons, dropped bombs on London, England, and pilots in German airplanes spied on the enemy. The United States had to catch up. To make this possible, President Woodrow Wilson established the National Advisory Committee for Aeronautics (NACA) in 1915. By 1917, construction had begun on an army airfield across the river from Norfolk, Virginia. NACA's laboratory within this development was known as Langley Memorial Aeronautical Laboratory, or Langley. NACA was given the task of using a scientific approach to developing aircraft.

Using Wind Tunnels

Many Americans' belief about flying was true. It was incredibly dangerous, especially for the pilots. Because of this, finding a scientific way to improve aircraft was vital. NACA would have to develop a reliable way to test aircraft and gather information on these tests. The agency could use this data to improve aircraft, but the data had to be collected first.

One possibility for data collection was to observe planes in flight. This meant the aircraft had to be flown in an area with cloudless skies that was far away from possible spies. Building aircraft and observing them as

Wind tunnels made testing aircraft easier and safer than flying.

part of a scientific test was expensive, and it was very
risky. On a good day, an aircraft that failed to perform
as predicted might be difficult to control, or it would not
get up to speed as quickly as predicted. On a bad day, the
failure of an experimental flight meant a crash, destroying
the plane and often killing the pilot.

Fortunately, it is possible to test an aircraft without actually flying it. Pieces of planes, such as wings or propellers, can be tested, as can scale models of planes. In either case, these tests take place in a structure called a wind channel or wind tunnel. The first wind tunnel was built in Langley in 1920. The tunnel was shaped like a tube, and powerful fans created the wind that duplicated the wind aircraft encounter during flight.

Instruments mounted on the models take readings during these tests. Scientists use data from the readings to tell if the aircraft is performing as expected or needs improvement. One of these instruments is a manometer. It measures air pressure. Air pressure varies based on altitude. But, more important for aircraft, air pressure is

THE CHALLENGES OF WORKING IN THE TUNNELS

Reading instruments in the wind tunnels was not a comfortable, easy assignment. The work was stressful, in part because the tunnels were stuffy and dark. The women had to move about on catwalks and take the readings as quickly as possible.

Mary Jackson's work as an engineer went beyond reading manometers or other instruments. After being hired as a mathematician in 1951, she worked inside the tunnels while they were in use, the fans roaring, so she could use a wrench to make small adjustments to the nuts in the aircraft part that was being tested. Jackson later suffered hearing loss and wondered if her work in the wind tunnels had contributed to it.

based on the movement of air across the surface of a wing or propeller.

Initially, engineers at Langley recorded the manometer data. This was a two-person job, with one person taking the reading and the other writing it down. The pair worked in a small, dark, stuffy area. Once the data was collected, the engineers ran the manometer readings through various equations to determine if the planes or parts had functioned as planned. If not, the engineers made changes and ran the tests again.

To make data analysis more efficient, NACA brought in workers to collect and process the data. These computers were all women, and their supervisors praised the women for doing more in a morning than an engineer could do in a day. The women did more than record numbers. They determined trajectories and performed other calculations using the data gathered during wind tunnel tests. They worked with the manometer data just as the engineers did. Their efforts freed the engineers to do other work and made the research process more efficient.

Another War, More Opportunities

The work of these women computers became even more important during World War II. This was the first war with serious aerial combat, making aircraft innovations more important than ever. In addition to working with aircraft, computers were needed to calculate the trajectories for the big guns used to bomb the enemy from a distance.

With men fighting in the war, NACA had to hire a new group of workers. In 1941, President Franklin Delano Roosevelt signed Executive Order 8802, desegregating the defense industry. This meant African Americans would work in all new defense areas. Starting in the winter of 1943, groups of computers worked across the United States running numbers that could help win the war. NACA's Langley facility was home to at least a dozen computing groups, ranging from one woman working alone to ten women working together. By 1943, Langley had a pool of African-American women it had recruited from black colleges across the United States. Men were generally engineers because the pay was better.

Mechanical Calculation

The women in this pool did more than basic calculations. Holes in the leading edge of aircraft wings and nose cones contained manometers. When the pressure on the aircraft changed, a mirror would flip in the manometer. The resulting flash of light was recorded on a strip of photosensitive tape. The computers read the tape and made the calculations needed to convert the data from the tape to something engineers could use.

Each tape included a series of vertical lines and several horizontal lines. The vertical lines marked the time. Some of the horizontal lines represented actual data. Others were for reference. The computer used a handheld tool called a film reader to measure the change between the actual data

MATHEMATICS AT WAR

When a World War II soldier needed to fire an artillery shell and hit a target that was one mile (1.6 km) away, he needed to know the angle of reach, or the angle at which to fire the shell and have it reach the target. An artillery shell travels in an arc toward the target. To calculate the angle of reach, the soldier needed to know the speed of the shell when fired, the sine for that speed, and the maximum height of the arc. The calculations were—and are—possible, but they are tricky, especially when the enemy may be firing at the soldier. Because of this, human computers did the math and compiled tables for soldiers to use in the field. Using the table for a particular big gun, the soldier would use the distance to find the angle required to hit the target.

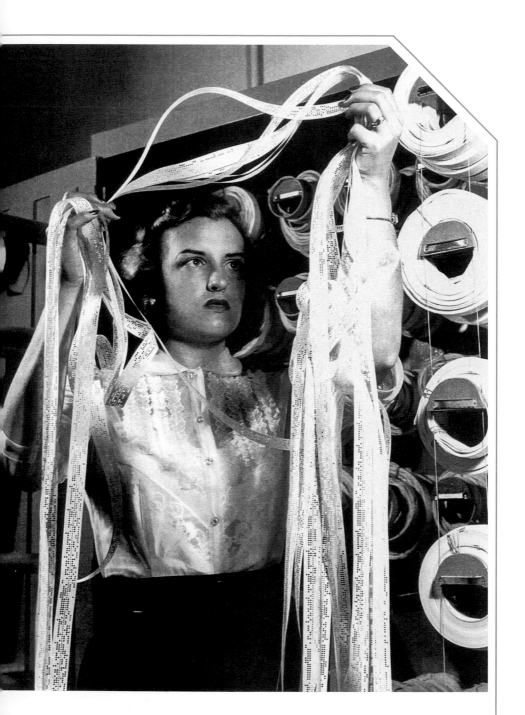

Human computers used data on the tape to make important calculations.

recorded and the reference line. Using these numbers to generate the information needed required a slide rule, a ruler-like device with a sliding center section used to quickly multiply and divide. The women computers also used a mechanical calculator, tables for the mathematical values sine and cosine, and standard atmosphere tables, which detail how air pressure changes at different altitudes. To read the tape, a computer used a magnifying glass to carefully examine the photosensitive strip of paper.

COMPUTING WITH A SLIDE RULE

Computers and engineers used slide rules to add and subtract, multiply and divide, find square roots, and do other sophisticated calculations. Slide rules are rectangular and about the size of a ruler. Divided into thirds, the top and bottom are fixed in place, but the middle section slides left and right. Each section has scales—numbers and line marks for calculations. For example, to multiply 3 x 3, slide the center of the slide rule so the 1 on the left end lines up with the 3 on the lower fixed ruler. Now look at the scale on the sliding rule. Find the 3 and look directly beneath it to find the answer: 9.

It takes time and patience to make calculations on a slide rule. In 1972, Hewlett-Packard released the first handheld electronic calculator. Practically overnight, modern technology replaced the slide rule.

Joining NACA

During World War II and after, as women continued making advances in education, working women were encouraged to become nurses and teachers. Some of the

Though outdated today, the slide rule was a crucial tool to NASA's computers.

women who worked at NACA had worked as teachers. These women and others often became NACA computers because they had people who encouraged them to study mathematics and use their knowledge in the workplace. One of these women was Katherine Johnson.

Johnson's father was a farmer and a janitor. Her mother was a teacher. Johnson loved numbers from an early age. "I counted everything. I counted the steps to the road, the steps up to church, the number of dishes and silverware I washed . . . anything that could be counted, I did," said Johnson.[1] But her hometown, White Sulphur Springs, West Virginia, limited education for African-American children to the eighth grade. To provide his smart daughter with greater opportunities for education, Johnson's father moved the family to Independence, West Virginia. There, Johnson graduated from high school at the young age of 14. Excited to study math in high school, Johnson found an encouraging mentor in her geometry teacher. Johnson studied hard and graduated early, entering college when she was only 15 years old.

At West Virginia State College in the 1930s, Johnson struggled to choose a major. She was considering English, French, and mathematics when one of her professors sought her out. "If you don't show up for my class, I will come and find you," joked the mathematics professor.[2] Johnson chose to major in math, following the advice of the professor who was so enthusiastic to have her as a student.

Other professors also encouraged Johnson. One of them, Dr. William

"My early memories are of my mother talking about doing math problems all day. Back then, all of the math was done with a #2 pencil and the aid of a slide rule. I remember the talk of plotting graphs, logs, doing equations and all sorts of foreign sounding terms."[3]

—Miriam Mann Harris on Miriam D. Mann's work at NACA

Katherine Johnson in 1971, during her long, successful career at NASA,
which began with working as a human computer

W. Schiefflin Claytor, realized how bright she was and how much she loved mathematics. "You'd make a great research mathematician," he said.[4] But he did not stop there. When he saw she had taken all the mathematics classes the college offered, he created a class in analytic geometry of space to help her expand her knowledge and follow her passion. After college, Johnson worked as a teacher. She gave that up when she married in 1939 and started a family. But she went back to work in 1953 when she joined the pool of African-American women computers.

Another woman who was encouraged to study mathematics was Christine Darden. Darden grew up interested in how things worked. Instead of playing with the dolls she was given, Darden took them apart and then put them back together. On weekends, she helped her father work on the family car. When Darden took high school geometry, she realized how much she loved math and decided she would study it when she enrolled at Hampton Institute in 1958. Her

"Both my parents felt very strongly about the value of education. I don't remember it being discussed a lot, but everybody in the house grew up knowing that they were going to college. Being much younger, I saw all my sisters and brothers go off to college."[5]

—Christine Darden

father encouraged this and advised her to become a math teacher so she could support herself. And she did.

While working as a teacher, Darden took weekend classes at Virginia State College. One of Darden's professors helped her find a job as a research assistant in aerosol physics, the study of things that contain both solids and liquids, such as smog. A year and a half later, someone at the college gave her an application to apply for a job at NACA, which had become the National Aeronautics and Space Administration (NASA) by then. Despite her experience in physics, she was assigned to the computing pool in 1967. She accepted the job, eager to put her knowledge of math and science to work.

All of the women who found a place among the African-American computers of NACA received encouragement. Some were cheered on by a parent. Others found their ally in a high school teacher. Still others were guided by college professors. The luckiest ones were encouraged at multiple levels. No matter who gave them the encouragement, they all found a place making history at NACA and NASA.

Christine Darden worked with NASA's wind tunnels for years and was photographed here in 1975.

CHAPTER FIVE

SEGREGATED SCIENCE

In 1950, NACA purchased the property where it built Langley. Until that time, the land was legally the Chesterville Plantation. Plantations were sprawling farms located in Southern states, worked by enslaved Africans and African Americans. These slaves were among the ancestors of the black women who came to NACA during World War II to work as computers.

NACA Wants You

With the war effort, NACA needed to expand its number of employees and expand fast. The organization set out to recruit bright young minds in chemistry and mathematics. They recruited not only to fill the greater need

An artist's rendering of Chesterville Plantation, which once occupied the site where the US government built Langley Research Center

made by the war but also to fill slots left open when male workers went to war. To find female workers, Langley advertised jobs in trade journals and sent pamphlets to colleges and universities. These recruiters, some of whom were NACA engineers, visited a variety of campuses. Women also heard about jobs at Langley through friends, relatives, and fellow students. This expansion included the computing pool, which branched out from the central pool. NACA also created additional pools in the main wind tunnels and the research divisions.

SEGREGATION AND JIM CROW LAWS

When Southern state legislatures passed segregation laws in the late 1800s, these laws were called Jim Crow laws. Some of these laws made it legal to keep black people out of white schools and libraries. The laws often left black public services underfunded. This left Jim Crow public libraries stocked with secondhand books. Jim Crow laws separated blacks from whites and ensured blacks only had access to inferior services.

NACA hired white women and black women, and all applicants for the computer jobs had to pass the civil service examination to be hired. Similar to the Jim Crow laws black voters faced in the South, an additional requirement was imposed on black women who wanted to work as computers. In addition to passing the test, the women had to pass a chemistry class at Hampton Institute. Even Miriam Daniel Mann, who already had a degree in chemistry, had to meet this requirement.

The organization did not always realize someone it had hired was black until the person arrived to start work. This was the case with Kathryn Peddrew.

Peddrew was born in Martinsburg, West Virginia. Her parents taught her she could be whatever she wanted to be, but she quickly realized the world put limitations on her as a black woman. She had majored in chemistry and tried several times to find a research position. One of her professors went to New Guinea to study quinine deafness. Quinine is the medication most commonly given to malaria patients. The medicine causes patients to lose their ability to hear high-pitched tones. Peddrew wanted to work on this project but discovered no women would be accepted because no plans had been made to house them separately from the men.

CIVIL SERVICE EXAMS

Civil service exams are given in various countries around the world. These tests are designed to ensure the people hired for government jobs are qualified and not simply getting the job based on who they know. It was not just the black computers who had to pass this exam or even the computers in general. Scientists and engineers as well as astronauts and pilots must pass a civil service exam, even today.

Although she was disappointed, she read a NACA bulletin and saw they were hiring employees in the chemistry division. She applied for a job and was hired. When she arrived on site in 1943, NACA personnel told Peddrew she could not work in chemistry because that particular division did not employ African Americans. NACA moved her to the computing division and placed her in the all-black West Building.

Katherine Peddrew worked at NACA and NASA for more than 40 years, though not in the position she was originally hired to do.

Separate but Not Equal

NACA was willing to give black women opportunities they might not otherwise have, but these women were not considered equal to their white counterparts. They could work only in certain areas and even had their own building. People renamed the group based on the name of the building. Their unit was known as "West Area Computing," and they were called "West Area Computers" or simply "West Computers."[1] Members of the group included Kathryn Peddrew, Dorothy Vaughan, Mary Jackson, and Miriam Daniel Mann.

The women faced segregation in other areas as well. In the cafeteria, they had to sit at tables with a sign that said "colored." Despite the segregation, the women had no complaints about the work itself. If one section had

VOTER DISCRIMINATION

Before taking a job with NACA in Iowa, Annie Easley dealt with Jim Crow laws when she registered to vote in Birmingham, Alabama. She described her experience: "Where I came from, in order to vote, you had to take a test and pay a poll tax. We had to literally take a test before we could register to vote, and as soon as I turned twenty-one, . . . I went down to vote, to sign up . . . I'd studied, I knew all of my Alabama history, and the test-giver looked at my application and said, 'You went to Xavier University. Two dollars.' He never asked me one question. But after that, I started to help train people to prepare for the test for voting."[2]

DOUBLE JEOPARDY

Gendered racism encompasses what is known as "double jeopardy."[4] Double jeopardy happens when someone is discriminated against for two reasons. Sometimes, it is difficult for a black woman to know if she is being treated badly because she is a woman (women cannot be junior engineers) or because she is black (black people cannot be chemists). She is both a woman and black. These traits intersect with one another—she is not one or the other but both.

more work than it could finish by a particular deadline, another section would help. This meant West Area Computers sometimes worked with their white counterparts, creating limited and temporary desegregation. The women noted that everyone worked together well, and there did not seem to be any bad feelings from the white computers or white male engineers. Although the West Area Computers worked with their white counterparts, not all the white computers realized there were black women doing this same job. The black computers remained invisible.

Despite the discrimination, both the

Working as a NASA computer allowed Miriam Daniel Mann, *second from right*, to help support her middle-class family.

white and black women were happy to have these jobs. This was the first chance many of these black women had to do more with their mathematics degrees than teach. Although they did the same work as male junior engineers who earned a starting salary of $2,600 per year, the women, both white and black, were classified as subprofessionals while the engineers were professionals.[5] This meant the women made only $1,440 per year as junior computers.[6] It was not fair, but it was more than they would have made teaching, which was approximately $550 per year.[7]

COLORED DINING

When people think of segregated dining facilities, they often think of the lunch counter protests in Greensboro, North Carolina. The protests took place after a small group of black students read Martin Luther King Jr.'s *Stride toward Freedom*, which is about the bus boycott in Montgomery, Alabama. These students started a sit-in at the restaurant at their local Woolworth's store, which had a policy of not serving black people. Later that month, college students staged a sit-in at a Woolworth's lunch counter in Nashville, Tennessee. Civil rights activist Stokely Carmichael said,

> *When I first heard about the Negroes sitting in at lunch counters down South, I thought they were just a bunch of publicity hounds. But one night when I saw those young kids on TV, getting back up on the lunch counter stools after being knocked off them, sugar in their eyes, ketchup in their hair—well, something happened to me. Suddenly I was burning.*[8]

The black women at NASA ate in the colored dining room, which was separated from the white dining room by the kitchen. Researchers know there was a "colored" sign that marked the area. What is not known is how the women felt about eating in a segregated dining room even as they worked for a desegregated organization.

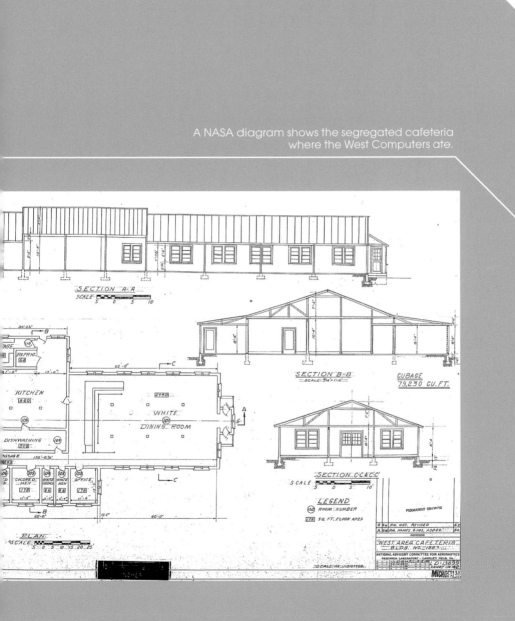

CHAPTER SIX

CHALLENGING THE SPACE RACE

The situation improved for the black computers after the Soviet Union launched *Sputnik* on October 4, 1957. *Sputnik* was the first satellite launched into Earth's orbit, and it had been sent into space by a Cold War enemy. The United States was not officially at war with the Soviet Union, but the two countries often worked against each other.

With this Soviet accomplishment, the space race was on. The US government wanted scientists to meet and do better than the Soviets. In part, this was a matter of technological pride. The United States did not want to be second best. It was also a matter of fear. If the Soviets could launch a satellite,

Visitors to an exhibit in Russia get an up-close view of *Sputnik III*.

US government officials worried the superpower would also be able to launch a nuclear strike. Space science could easily be used in weapons, and being second best could mean losing a war against the Soviets.

The United States needed to move forward fast, so one of the nation's scientific centers, NACA, was transformed into the National Air and Space Administration (NASA) in October 1958. The name change reflected a change in focus from air flight to space exploration.

To catch up to the Soviets, Americans who were interested and had the right skills needed to be educated in science. To make this happen, Congress passed the National Defense Education Act in August 1958. Under the act, the federal government made loans and scholarships available to qualified students to study math and science.

The United States also needed to make the best possible use of those who already had a science education. To do this, NASA needed to use its resources well and end segregation. Among other changes, this meant no longer keeping the black computers separate in the West Building. But while this was a step in the right direction, it did not end unfair practices. As Easley explained, NASA was made up of many of the same people who had worked at NACA. There was no Equal Opportunity Office to go to if there was a problem. It was up to individual managers to take action if and when something happened. Easley said,

> People don't change. . . . Some of those people stayed around for a long time, and some of their behavior was passed on to other people. I think of the poem 'Mother to Son.' 'Life for me ain't been no crystal stair,' but you got to keep struggling. You keep going because you want to.[1]

By this time, the late 1950s, NASA was employing even more black women. These women worked not only to meet the new US goal to reach space but also to achieve something closer to equality.

Challenging the Status Quo

Working toward equality meant challenging the status quo and changing the way things were done. Katherine Johnson had always been outspoken, and she did not change when she began to work at NACA in 1953. She was assigned to the all-male flight research division. Shortly after she took the job, Johnson noticed the men would all attend informational meetings called briefings. She was not invited to these briefings even though she worked with the same information as the men. When she asked about it, her supervisor explained women did not attend these meetings. Johnson asked if there was a law against it. When she learned there was not, Johnson began attending the meetings. "I asked questions, I wanted to know why," Johnson told a NASA interviewer. "They got used to me asking questions and being the only woman there."[2]

NACA hired Dorothy Vaughan in 1943. In 1949, NACA promoted Vaughan, making her supervisor of the West Area Computers. Not only was she the first black woman to supervise these black computers, she was also the first black manager in NACA's history. But even with black managers, change did not come easily. "I changed what I could, and what I couldn't, I endured," said Vaughan.[3]

Other computers sought to advance by becoming engineers. One of the first was Mary Jackson. Jackson began working at NACA in 1951 as a West Computer. She took classes at the University of Virginia and qualified to

Dorothy Vaughan, *left*, became a computer programmer and worked at NASA until 1971.

work as an aerospace engineer in 1958, the year NACA became NASA. She told interviewers she would not have succeeded if her boss had not mentored her, encouraging her and giving her advice.

Christine Darden followed a similar path. Darden worked as a computer for eight years, beginning in 1967, but after wading through calculations for that long, she was ready to say something to her supervisor. She had been taking engineering classes through Langley and noted she did as well, if not better, than her classmates, who were mostly white male engineers.

Darden pointed out to her supervisor that she had a master's degree in engineering. She wanted to know why other people with her degree were working as engineers while she was still a computer. Darden's supervisor was impressed by her work and transferred her to an engineering section in 1973. Darden was one of the few women at that time who worked as an aerospace engineer

Christine Darden published her work with sonic booms.

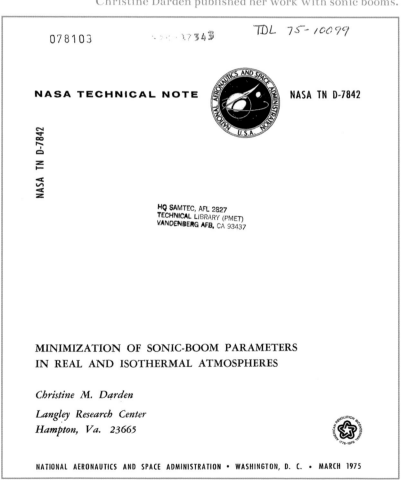

078103   ·⁙· ⵉ7343   TDL 75-10099

NASA TECHNICAL NOTE   NASA TN D-7842

NASA TN D-7842

HQ SAMTEC, AFL 2827
TECHNICAL LIBRARY (PMET)
VANDENBERG AFB, CA 93437

MINIMIZATION OF SONIC-BOOM PARAMETERS
IN REAL AND ISOTHERMAL ATMOSPHERES

Christine M. Darden

Langley Research Center
Hampton, Va. 23665

NATIONAL AERONAUTICS AND SPACE ADMINISTRATION • WASHINGTON, D. C. • MARCH 1975 at Langley. Her work involved reducing sonic booms in supersonic aircraft, which travel faster than the speed of sound.

Rough Waters

While new policies should have enabled the women to get ahead in their careers, things did not always go smoothly. Starting in the 1970s, NASA began paying for undergraduate coursework that was job related. Easley wanted to take math classes at nearby Cuyahoga Community College. She went to her supervisor, Bert Henry, to see if NASA would pay for the classes. He told her NASA did not pay for such courses.

Easley tried to explain that she knew they had given other people aid for education. Henry said,

SONIC BOOM

A sonic boom is the thundering sound of the airwaves created when anything, including a plane, moves faster than the speed of sound. A larger, heavier plane pushes aside more air, so the sonic boom it creates is stronger than that caused by a smaller plane. Because people worry about the damage to both buildings and human beings caused by these booms, more than 50 countries have laws against commercial supersonic aircraft flying over their territory. Christine Darden was one of the engineers who tried to reduce these booms. Darden worked on how to predict sonic booms and how to minimize them. She also worked on the wing design and flap design for planes flying at supersonic speeds. Darden's work in this field included writing computer code. All sonic boom minimization work since the 1970s has used Darden's code.

"They only do it for professionals."[4] She showed him the college flyer that stated NASA paid for classes, but his mind was made up. Easley paid for her own classes.

One of the engineers heard about Easley's situation. He told her it was ridiculous she had been unable to get help and spoke to someone in the training department. He explained that Easley did not want to cause problems and had tried to go through her supervisor, which is what she was supposed to do. When Easley finished the class she was taking at the time, she turned in her grade to the training department. A woman from that department contacted Easley's supervisor: "I see that Annie took a math course. Why didn't she come to us for financial aid?"[5] The woman then told Easley NASA had helped a lot of people and would help her, too.

Easley eventually decided it would be easiest to finish college if she was not working full time. She knew of one NASA employee who had taken a paid leave. She went to the training department and asked for the same thing, but they turned her down and said no one had ever been given that opportunity. Easley knew this was untrue but took an unpaid leave to finish her degree. NASA was so slow to approve her leave that she had been taking a class two weeks before it was finally approved. Easley was determined to forge ahead and refused to let anyone stop her. She graduated from Cleveland State University in 1977 with a bachelor's degree in mathematics.

Equal Opportunities

Fortunately, other people working at NASA were good at figuring out what it took to get ahead. Jackson was one of them. Despite the impressive work Jackson did in aerodynamics, she is best known for her efforts in fighting for equal opportunity.

Jackson realized minorities and women at NASA did not always get promotions as quickly as they should. She took a careful look at what might be holding them back. Sometimes, they were not quite as well educated as other workers, lacking just a few classes. Other times, they worked in a division that was sometimes overlooked, or they did not work on attention-getting assignments. She also noted how women were often stopped short from advancing in their jobs largely because they were women.

Jackson spoke with her female coworkers about the classes they needed to take and the degrees they needed

Mary Jackson's long career with NASA included working in the organization's affirmative action program, providing employees the support she did not have when she was a computer.

to earn to become engineers instead of computers. She was one of the first women to become a NASA engineer. Others saw her progress and followed in her footsteps. Although Jackson enjoyed engineering, she applied for a position in equal opportunity. After being trained in Washington, DC, Jackson returned to Langley in 1979 and worked as an affirmative action program manager and federal women's program manager. She was able to make changes that helped minorities and assist managers in noting the accomplishments of their minority and female employees.

CHAPTER SEVEN

RACE, PLACE, AND OUTER SPACE

By 1962, when astronaut John Glenn was ready to make his record-setting Mercury flight to leave the atmosphere and orbit Earth, NASA had an electronic computer that filled an entire room. Computing was ready to move into the electronic age, but the astronauts were not ready to trust machines to do the job. One mathematical error could mean failing to reenter Earth's atmosphere and death for the men in the capsule. Glenn did not want to trust his life to an electronic computer. The launch had already been canceled five times because of weather and equipment

John Glenn, with the craft in which he orbited the Earth, owes his success in part to the work of Katherine Johnson and other women computers.

failures, so tensions surrounding the mission were high. Glenn wanted one person in particular to verify the data from the electronic computer.

At Glenn's request, NASA called Katherine Johnson to do the job. NASA wanted Glenn's capsule to land in a specific place in the ocean. If it struck land, he would die. If it approached Earth at too shallow an angle, it would bounce off the planet's atmosphere. When asked about her calculations years later, Johnson explained that the trajectory, or path, followed by the Mercury module was an arc. All she had to do was calculate where the capsule would be at any given time. The calculations were tricky because Johnson had to factor in the rotation of the Earth, but she had years of experience doing similar computations. Her calculations verified the information the computer produced.

Code It

Although people did not yet trust the data electronic computers produced, it did not take long for them to realize the machines were quicker and more efficient than even the hardest-working human computer. As electronic computers began taking over the job of computation, the role of the human beings shifted to programming. These women wrote the programs and manuals that allowed computers to take over their jobs.

Electronic computers are programmed using languages created specifically to communicate instructions to these machines. Many of the women working at NASA used FORTRAN, which is short for "formula translation." FORTRAN was created for use by engineers, mathematicians, and scientists. One of the oldest programming languages, FORTRAN was written to be easy to understand and debug, which is the process of discovering and removing errors from a new program. Vaughan explained that FORTRAN was easy for

WRITING FORTRAN

When NASA's former human computers started programming electronic computers in FORTRAN, programs were not saved electronically on computer disks. They were saved on punch cards. Each of these lightweight cardboard cards contained a single line of code. Holes were punched in different patterns in each row, with each pattern representing a specific character. Converting information from a written program to punched cards could be confusing, so programmers wrote their programs on special paper forms with columns that corresponded to the columns on the cards.

the women to learn because it was based on algebra, a kind of math. Once the former computers had mastered it, they taught it to the engineers.

THE CENTAUR

Easley played an important part at NASA by writing the code for the Centaur rocket. Known as NASA's "Workhorse in Space," the Centaur rocket first launched in 1963.[2] This high-energy rocket propelled a variety of satellites and exploratory craft into space. For the two Viking missions in the mid-1970s, a Centaur rocket took an unmanned craft to the surface of Mars. Each of the two Viking missions was intended to last for 90 days after landing, the length of time the two landers were expected to transmit data to Earth. The first lasted for four years. The second lasted for two years. In 1977, the Centaur also took the Voyager probes into space to send back information about Jupiter and Saturn. Both of the crafts functioned longer than expected and were still transmitting in 2016. The Centaur made both of these important and historic fact-finding missions possible.

Easley wrote the code for the Centaur rocket. Easley's work laid the foundation for the launches of weather, military, and communications satellites as well as space shuttle launches. The programs Easley and Vaughan wrote were not for a one-time use. These talented African-American women were doing the groundwork that would keep the United States in space.

Energize Me

In addition to programming, these women also helped develop other technologies that would be used in space and on Earth. A big part

SCIENCE and ENGINEERING
NEWSLETTER

MS. ANNIE J. EASLEY, MATHEMATICIAN
LEWIS RESEARCH CENTER
NATIONAL AERONAUTICS & SPACE ADMINISTRATION

NASA featured Annie Easley on the cover of an issue of its publication
Science and Engineering Newsletter.

of space exploration and travel is energy, ranging from how to access energy while in space to how to use it most efficiently. Boosting rocket fuel into space is one of the greatest costs of any launch. Because of this, NASA scientists have worked to use energies available in space.

Part of Easley's work involved developing batteries for electric vehicles such as the Mars rovers. She also helped harness wind and sunlight to make their energies available for use when needed. Finally, she focused on determining how to tell how much energy was present and how to use it most effectively. Easley's work was not only used in space. It can also be found in the batteries used in hybrid cars.

Not Enough Progress

Some people believed the US government placed too much emphasis on space flight. They thought the money and work dedicated to space exploration should go toward improving the situation of those who lived in poverty.

Even though the government created the Freedmen's Bureau to improve the lives of impoverished blacks following the end of slavery, many blacks still failed to get an education. Part of the problem was that schools often turned away black students, even those who were qualified to attend. That was the case in 1963 when two black students were supposed to be admitted to the University of Alabama. This event led to President John F. Kennedy's televised address in which he discussed the perils discrimination posed to the country. "A great change is at hand, and our task, our obligation, is to make that revolution, that change a peaceful one," said Kennedy.[3] Fortunately, positive changes were occurring, and NASA was leading the way. This was the time when NASA recruited mathematician Christine Darden from Virginia State University. Things were far from perfect, but the women computers of NASA were a symbol of what could be.

"WHITEY ON THE MOON"

One NASA critic was author and musician Gil Scott-Heron, who wrote the song "Whitey on the Moon." In the song, Scott-Heron highlights the negative experiences of many African Americans. He also emphasizes the great attention and resources given to the space program through the single, repeated line, "Whitey on the moon." He begins,

A rat done bit my sister Nell
With Whitey on the moon
Her face and arms began
to swell
And Whitey's on the moon[4]

After describing poor living conditions and lack of money, partially due to increased taxes to pay for space flight, Scott-Heron returns to the sister bitten by a rat. He then ends the song by stating he has had enough and he'll send the doctor bills "airmail special / To Whitey on the moon."[5]

CHAPTER EIGHT

SCIENCE
IN SPACE

In the late 1950s, NASA began taking flight in a new direction. The organization was focused on space flight, and its success would rely on women. Initial achievements were made using calculations by West Computers. Later success came on the heels of women who challenged the limits others placed on them.

In January 1958, NASA began reviewing the records of 508 military test pilots, looking for men to become the nation's first astronauts.[1] The agency selected 110 candidates in 1959.[2] So many of these men volunteered for astronaut training the training slots were filled before the last third were ever contacted. NASA chose to train test pilots

Mae C. Jemison made history when she achieved her dream of becoming an astronaut.

WOMEN TAKE THE FIRST ASTRONAUT TESTS

Dr. William Lovelace was a surgeon in the Army Medical Corps Reserve when he developed an oxygen flight mask for flight personnel. He had left the military and opened a clinic in New Mexico when NASA invited him to help develop the tests the first male astronauts had to pass to gain access to space. He wanted to know how women would fare taking these same tests. In 1960, he invited pilot Jerrie Cobb to endure the same training and tests as the men. Cobb was the first woman to pass the testing, and she recruited other women to train. Although 13 women passed the initial stages in testing for endurance, vertigo, and nerve response, the program was canceled. It had been funded privately without NASA backing, and NASA refused to train the women for space because they were not military test pilots.

because these men had already demonstrated their ability to withstand the physical and psychological strain of a dangerous job.

The decision to train military test pilots made sense, but it barred those not allowed to fly for the military, primarily women. The women computers had shown NASA they were valuable team members. During World War II, they had worked six-day work weeks. They even worked on Sundays as needed. But without experience as military pilots, women remained earthbound. This changed in 1977 when NASA selected 200 new astronaut candidates. These astronauts would train for space shuttle missions. Each shuttle crew would consist of seven people, but only two needed to be trained pilots. These two astronauts would still be military pilots. The other five astronauts could have backgrounds in science, engineering, or medicine. They would conduct scientific experiments in space.

Of the 200 candidates chosen for training in 1977, six were women.[3] Among these women was astrophysicist Sally Ride, a scientist who studied the physical properties of stars and other objects in space. On June 18, 1983, she flew into space and became the first female US astronaut.

Ten Years In

On June 4, 1987, ten years after Ride entered astronaut training, Mae C. Jemison became the first African-American woman admitted into the training program. Jemison was born in Decatur, Alabama, in 1956. Just as Johnson's father moved her family so she could have greater opportunities for education, Jemison's parents moved the family to Chicago, Illinois, when she was three years old. There, their children could receive a better education. Throughout school, Jemison studied science. After high school, she entered Stanford University. She graduated in 1977 with degrees in chemical engineering and African and Afro-American studies. Next, Jemison studied medicine. She became a medical doctor in 1981. Working with the Peace Corps, she often traveled to Sierra Leone and Liberia, two countries in West Africa, to conduct research and teach medicine.

When she returned to the United States, Jemison applied to become an astronaut. She had enjoyed studying space in high school and wanted the chance to learn about it firsthand. In 1987, she was one of 15 people chosen from approximately 2,000 candidates.[4] She finished her training in approximately one year, becoming a science mission specialist. This meant she would perform crew-related science experiments on a mission.

"Once I got into space, I was feeling very comfortable in the universe. I felt like I had a right to be anywhere in this universe, that I belonged here as much as any speck of stardust, any comet, any planet."[5]

—Mae Carol Jemison, the first female African-American astronaut

Jemison would have the opportunity to conduct tests in space. This was an opportunity her human computer predecessors, such as Christine Darden, could only have imagined. While Darden was limited to testing sonic boom minimization through the computer programs she had written, Jemison was going to fly in a craft that would create those booms.

On September 12, 1992, Jemison flew into space aboard the *Endeavour* space shuttle. She studied the effects of weightlessness and motion sickness on the crew, including herself. She also did two experiments on bone cells, a vital field of study because astronauts lose bone mass while in space and can develop brittle bones. She returned to Earth eight days later.

Small in Number

Today, more than 25 years after Jemison was selected for astronaut training, only five black women have qualified as astronauts. Joan Higginbotham, Yvonne Cagle, and Stephanie D. Wilson were next. They joined the program in August 1996.

Before becoming an astronaut, Higginbotham was a NASA engineer who took part in 53 space shuttle launches.[6] Unlike many astronauts, she did not dream of working in space exploration. Her plan was to earn a degree in electrical engineering

ASTRONAUT STATUSES

Astronauts have a variety of classifications depending on whether or not they are "mission ready," or ready and awaiting an assignment.[7] Active astronauts such as Stephanie D. Wilson are ready and able to take on a mission if NASA assigns one to them. Other astronauts, including Mae C. Jemison, are listed as former astronauts, meaning they have retired and no longer work with NASA. Yvonne Cagle is a management astronaut. She is no longer ready to fly a mission, but she still works at NASA. Whether or not they are still ready to fly into space, many NASA astronauts work to help the United States advance in space science.

Stephanie D. Wilson, *center*, on the International Space Station in April 2010

and work for IBM, a computer and technology company. When she graduated in 1987, IBM was not hiring, but NASA offered her a job. She applied twice to astronaut training school before she was accepted. Her primary role was as a robotic arm operator. She operated the controls that move the arm, supporting beams, and other massive components. She maneuvered the equipment within inches of other pieces without collisions.

Cagle earned a degree in biochemistry from San Francisco State University in 1981 and a medical degree from the University of Washington in 1985. Certified in aerospace medicine, she served in the US Air Force as the medical liaison to an *Atlantis* space shuttle mission in

1989 before training as an astronaut in 1996. She worked within the space shuttle and space station programs.

Stephanie D. Wilson became the fourth black female astronaut. She earned a bachelor's degree in engineering from Harvard University in 1988, then a master's degree in aerospace engineering from the University of Texas in 1992. She analyzed data concerning the accuracy of various elements of space flight, from spin rate to antennae pointing. In 1996, she reported for astronaut training. Her first assignment was in space station payload display and procedures. She has since performed technical tasks concerning space shuttle engines and rocket boosters.

Like Wilson, the fifth black female astronaut, Jeanette Epps, has a degree in aerospace engineering. She earned her doctorate at the University of Maryland in 2000. After graduation, she worked in Ford Motor Company's research department. In 2009, NASA chose Epps as a candidate for its twentieth astronaut class. She is scheduled to take part in a mission in 2018. She will spend six months on the International Space Station.

African-American women continue to make an impact in space exploration. They also help make their roles as engineers, scientists, and astronauts more visible to girls who are studying science and math today.

CHAPTER NINE
HIDDEN
NO MORE

While the United States is no longer in a space race, NASA officials know their organization needs to recruit the best and the brightest scientific minds, regardless of their race or gender, to continue innovating. Because of this, they are working to recruit more black women as well as people from other underrepresented groups. To accomplish this, NASA has not called on a black female scientist but a black actress who played a space explorer on television.

From 1966 to 1969, Nichelle Nichols starred in the original *Star Trek* television series as Lieutenant Uhura, the ship's communication officer. Her part was small, but it had a big

Although she is an actress and not a scientist, Nichelle Nichols has become a popular spokesperson for NASA.

impact, bringing a minority character onto the screen alongside white men. Just as her role on the popular television show drew attention, NASA officials knew Nichols would draw attention to their space program.

Nichols first recruited people for NASA in the 1970s and 1980s. She traveled to universities with strong science and engineering programs. She was even a guest at the North American Aerospace Defense Command, commonly referred to as NORAD. This US and Canadian organization is charged with monitoring and defending the air space over the two countries. Speaking about her visit there, Nichols pointed out that she went where "no civilian had gone before."[1]

Nichols's efforts ultimately recruited six female candidates and three African-American men, but that was not the end of her publicity for NASA.

UHURA'S IRONY

It was essential that Uhura be seen on the bridge because the *Star Trek* crew was from an advanced society that would not discriminate against a black woman. The irony is the studio that produced the show refused to give Nichols a contract. A contract for the series would have guaranteed Nichols a long-term role as Uhura. Instead, she was expected to show up daily and see if she had a role in that particular episode. The men who played Captain Kirk and Spock both had contracts. Thanks to Nichols's determination, Uhura's presence on the bridge inspired young black women to enter science and space.

On September 15, 2015, Nichols flew on board the Stratospheric Observatory for Infrared Astronomy (SOFIA), taking part in NASA's Airborne Astronomy Ambassadors Program. SOFIA consists of an infrared telescope on board a 747 jet aircraft that carries both the equipment and the observers into the upper reaches of Earth's atmosphere. The program is designed for teachers and science center educators. Nichols was included for her ability to encourage others in their pursuit of science.

"What was really great about *Star Trek* when I was growing up as a little girl is not only did they have Lt. Uhura played by Nichelle Nichols as a technical officer—she was African. At the same time, they had this crew that was composed of people from all around the world and they were working together to learn more about the universe, so that helped to fuel my whole idea that I could be involved in space exploration as well as in the sciences."[2]

—*Mae Carol Jemison*

Telling Their Story

While Nichols worked to recruit black women to NASA, historians worked to uncover the past. Perhaps the first researcher to write about the black computers was Dr. Beverly Golemba of Saint Leo College, which is on Virginia's Langley Air Force Base. Her paper, "Human Computers: The Women in Aeronautical Research," tells the history of Langley's computers. Golemba interviewed 13 of the women, including three of the black computers: Kathryn Peddrew, Dorothy Vaughan, and Mary Jackson. Golemba wrote about their work, their living and working conditions, and the issues facing black women at NACA. Because Golemba's manuscript was unpublished and not widely available, many people remained unaware of the role these women played.

Fortunately, Margot Lee Shetterly's work on the black women computers has made them much more visible. She wrote the book *Hidden Figures: The American Dream and the Untold Story of the Black Women Mathematicians Who Helped Win the Space Race*, published in 2016. In it, she highlights the work of five black women computers at NASA: Gloria Champine, Christine Darden, Mary Jackson, Katherine Johnson, and Dorothy Vaughan. These women worked on Friendship 7, the mission that sent astronaut John Glenn around the planet. The book was made into a film scheduled to be released in 2017.

In 2014, Margot Lee Shetterly gave a talk at Langley during Women's History Month.

The Human Computers at NASA project of Macalester College in Saint Paul, Minnesota, is also working to bring the stories of these women to light. The project is a joint effort between college students and faculty to create a single website for visitors to easily access online information about the African-American women computers. The project website provides links to a variety of material, including interviews, newspaper articles, and images. Through this website, visitors can

BLACK GIRLS CODE

NASA not only honors yesterday's black female scientists but also works to inspire the scientists of tomorrow. Black Girls Code (BGC) is a not-for-profit organization that provides technology education to African-American girls ages seven to 17. Kimberly Bryant, an electrical engineer working in biotech for more than 20 years, founded BGC in 2011. Bryant spoke at the 2016 International Space Apps Challenge, a collaboration focused on space exploration. The two-day event takes place in cities around the world. NASA puts on these events, pairing with government organizations and more than 100 local teams worldwide.

see all these women did to bring the United States into space and to open the way for other black women at NASA and in the fields of science, technology, engineering, and mathematics.

NASA's Efforts

NASA is also sharing the stories of all its women computers. NASA librarians are working to preserve as much material about the human computers as possible. On the NASA website, librarians are archiving everything from photographs of the women to interviews with them. Brief biographies and a variety of scanned documents are also preserved for all to see.

Christine Darden, *left*, Katherine Johnson, *seated*, and other former Langley computers returned to Langley in 2014 to attend Margot Lee Shetterly's Women's History Month lecture.

NASA's efforts have not stopped with digital preservation. The organization has also honored one of the black women computers publicly. On May 5, 2016, the fifty-fifth anniversary of Alan Shepard's trip into space, NASA dedicated a new research facility in Langley: the Katherine G. Johnson Computational Research Facility. Johnson, who was 97 years old at the time, attended the event. She was the only original black human computer who lived to know their story would not remain hidden. Instead, the histories of these women are being brought into the light of day where they can continue to inspire.

TIMELINE

1700s
The first human computers worked in astronomy in Europe.

MID-1800s
The United States forms a computing group to create the *Nautical Almanac* for navigation.

1914–1918
During World War I, computers work for the military computing trajectories and other data. Many of these computers are white women.

1915
President Woodrow Wilson establishes the National Advisory Committee for Aeronautics (NACA).

1917
Construction begins on NACA's Langley Memorial Aeronautical Laboratory, or Langley.

1941
President Franklin Delano Roosevelt signs Executive Order 8802, desegregating the defense industry.

1943
Langley creates the first pool of African-American women computers; NACA hires Kathryn Peddrew for a job in chemistry but does not allow blacks to work in that area and transfers her to the computing division.

1951
NACA hires Mary Jackson as a mathematician, and she works in the wind tunnels.

1953
Katherine Johnson, a mathematician, becomes a computer at NACA.

1955
Annie Easley begins working in the Computer Service Division at NACA's Lewis Research Center.

1957
The Soviet Union sends *Sputnik* into space on October 4, launching the space race with the United States.

1958
NACA becomes the National Air and Space Administration (NASA) in October.

1960s

Easley writes the computer code for the Centaur rocket.

1962

American astronaut John Glenn refuses to go on his mission to orbit Earth until Johnson confirms calculations made by an electronic computer.

1967

Physicist Christine Darden becomes a computer at NASA.

1970s

Darden develops computer code that has been used in sonic boom minimization work ever since.

1979

After starting her career as a mathematician at Langley and becoming an aerospace engineer, Jackson becomes an affirmative action manager.

1987

On June 4, Mae C. Jemison becomes the first black woman to train as an astronaut.

1992

On September 12, Jemison becomes the first African-American woman in space.

2015

On February 6, Charles F. Bolden Jr., NASA administrator, publishes NASA's policy on equal employment opportunity, which stresses fairness and equity.

2016

NASA dedicates the Katherine G. Johnson Computational Research Facility on May 5.

ESSENTIAL FACTS

- The National Advisory Committee for Aeronautics (NACA) formed in 1915 and worked to scientifically design and test aircraft and help the United States catch up to more advanced European aviation.

- The National Aeronautics and Space Administration (NASA) was created in 1958 from NACA and emphasized space exploration rather than flight itself.

- Katherine Johnson is perhaps the most well known of the African-American women who worked as NACA and NASA computers. Her work was so well respected that in 1962, astronaut John Glenn refused to launch his craft into orbit until Johnson confirmed the data processed by the electronic computer.

- Mae C. Jemison became the first African-American woman astronaut in 1987 and the first black woman in space in 1992.

KEY EVENTS

- In 1962, Katherine Johnson calculated the trajectory the Mercury space capsule had to use to reenter the Earth's atmosphere. Her findings confirmed the information already provided by an electronic computer.

- In the 1960s, Annie Easley wrote the computer code used with the Centaur rocket. This code was the basis of later codes used in the space shuttle program and a variety of military, weather, and communications satellites.

- In 1987, Mae C. Jemison was accepted into NASA's astronaut training program and later became the first US black female astronaut. She accomplished this not as a former military pilot but as a doctor, teacher, and scientist.

IMPACT ON SOCIETY

- With the signing of Executive Order 8802 in 1941, President Franklin D. Roosevelt prohibited racial discrimination in the national defense industry. Although many areas would still be segregated, more opportunities opened up for African Americans, and black women were first hired as computers at NACA.

- Before NACA started hiring them as computers, black women with degrees in mathematics generally went into teaching. With NACA, and later NASA, these women had the chance to use their knowledge to carry the United States into space. These women were essential to US efforts in the space race, performing a wide variety of calculations, training and becoming engineers, and writing computer code and manuals. They led the way for black women and other minorities in the aerospace industry, including the first African-American women astronauts.

QUOTE

"You can be anything you want to. It doesn't matter what you look like, what your size is, what your color is. You can be anything you want to, but you do have to work at it."

—Annie Easley's mother to Annie Easley

GLOSSARY

AERONAUTICS
The science of airplanes and flight.

CELESTIAL
Of or relating to the sky and visible heavenly bodies.

COLD WAR
The political and military tension between the United States and the Soviet Union after World War II; a cold war does not have actual fighting.

COMPUTATION
The process of calculating something; doing math.

COMPUTER
Something or someone that performs calculations and handles data.

DISCRIMINATION
Unfair treatment of other people, usually because of race, age, or gender.

EQUAL OPPORTUNITY
Policies and practices in employment that do not discriminate against people on the basis of traits such as sex, race, or religion.

GRAVITATIONAL PULL

An invisible force something, such as a planet, has that draws other objects toward it.

PERIHELION

The point in a comet's or planet's orbit when it is closest to the sun.

SEGREGATION

The practice of separating groups of people based on race, gender, ethnicity, or other factors.

VERTIGO

Dizziness.

WIND TUNNEL

A tunnel for testing the effects of wind and air pressure on aircraft.

ADDITIONAL
RESOURCES

SELECTED BIBLIOGRAPHY

Fairfax, Colita Nichols. *Hampton, Virginia.* Mount Pleasant, SC: Arcadia, 2005. Print.

Golemba, Beverly E. "Human Computers: The Women in Aeronautical Research." *NASA,* NASA, 1995. Web. 7 June 2016.

Grier, David Alan. *When Computers Were Human.* Princeton, NJ: Princeton UP, 2007. Print.

FURTHER READINGS

Benoit, Peter. *The Space Race.* New York: Scholastic, 2012. Print.

Gibson, Karen Bush. *Women in Space.* Chicago: Chicago Review, 2014. Print.

Sullivan, Otha Richard. *African-American Women Scientists and Inventors.* San Francisco: Jossey-Bass, 2012. Print.

WEBSITES

To learn more about Hidden Heroes, visit **booklinks.abdopublishing.com**. These links are routinely monitored and updated to provide the most current information available.

FOR MORE INFORMATION

For more information on this subject, contact or visit the following organizations:

DEWITT WALLACE LIBRARY

Macalester College
1600 Grand Avenue
Saint Paul, MN 55105
651-696-6346
http://digitalcommons.macalester.edu/amst_humancomp/
Human Computers at NASA is a student-faculty collaborative project in Macalester's American Studies department. The project seeks to shed light on the buried stories of black women with math and science degrees who began working at NACA in 1943 in secret, segregated facilities.

HAMPTON HISTORY MUSEUM

120 Old Hampton Lane
Hampton, VA 23669
757-727-1610
http://www.hampton.gov/index.aspx?NID=119
This museum's exhibits include information on the first African-American settlement, the Grand Contraband Camp.

NASA

300 E Street SW, Suite 5R30
Washington, DC 20546
202-358-0001
http://www.nasa.gov/about/contact/index.html
NASA is continually updating its files about the women who have worked at the Langley Research Center and in other areas.

SOURCE NOTES

CHAPTER 1. NASA'S SECRET

1. "Annie J. Easley Interviewed by Sandra Johnson: Cleveland, Ohio—August 21, 2001." *Johnson Space Center*. National Aeronautics and Space Administration,16 July 2010. Web. 16 Sept. 2016.

2. Ibid.

3. Ibid.

4. Ibid.

5. "Human Computers." *NASA Cultural Resources (CRGIS)*. National Aeronautics and Space Administration, 3 May 2016. Web. 16 Sept. 2016.

6. "National Aeronautics and Space Administration Policy Statement on Equal Employment Opportunity." *NASA Headquarters*. National Aeronautics and Space Administration, 16 Feb. 2016. Web. 16 Sept. 2016.

7. "MannBio." *NASA Cultural Resources (CRGIS)*. National Aeronautics and Space Administration, 12 Sept. 2011. Web. 16 Sept. 2016.

CHAPTER 2. HUMAN COMPUTERS

1. "Maria Kirch." Encyclopædia Britannica. Encyclopædia Britannica, 2016. Web. 16 Sept. 2016.

2. "Chapter 18." *Literature Network*. Jalic, 2015. Web. 16 Sept. 2016.

3. David Alan Grier. *When Computers Were Human*. Princeton, NJ: Princeton UP, 2005. Print. 81–82.

4. Ibid.

5. David Skinner. "The Age of Female Computers." *New Atlantis*. Center for the Study of Technology and Society, Ethics and Public Policy Center, 2006. Web. 16 Sept. 2016.

CHAPTER 3. EDUCATING BLACK AMERICA

1. "Black Towns." *Encyclopedia.com*. Encyclopedia.com, 2006. Web. 16 Sept. 2016.

2. "Fort Monroe and the 'Contrabands of War.'" *National Park Service*. National Park Service, US Department of the Interior, n.d. Web. 15 Sept. 2016.

3. "Dr. Rebecca Lee Crumpler." *Changing the Face of Medicine*. National Library of Medicine, n.d. Web. 16 Sept. 2016.

4. David Conrads. "Josephine Silone Yates: Teacher, Journalist, and Clubwoman 1859–1912." *Kansas City Public Library*. Kansas City Public Library, 2009. Web. 15 Sept. 2016.

CHAPTER 4. FLIGHT AND FIGHT

1. "Katherine Johnson: A Lifetime of STEM." *NASA.* National Aeronautics and Space Administration, 6 Nov. 2013. Web. 15 Sept. 2016.

2. Ibid.

3. "MannBio." *NASA Cultural Resources (CRGIS).* National Aeronautics and Space Administration, 12 Sept. 2011. Web. 16 Sept. 2016.

4. "Katherine Johnson: A Lifetime of STEM." *NASA.* National Aeronautics and Space Administration, 6 Nov. 2013. Web. 15 Sept. 2016.

5. Wini Warren. *Black Women Scientists in the United States.* Bloomington: Indiana UP, 1999. Print. 75.

CHAPTER 5. SEGREGATED SCIENCE

1. "Dorothy Vaughn." *Human Computer Project.* Human Computer Project, n.d. Web. 16 Sept. 2016.

2. "Annie J. Easley Interviewed by Sandra Johnson: Cleveland, Ohio—August 21, 2001." *Johnson Space Center.* National Aeronautics and Space Administration,16 July 2010. Web. 16 Sept. 2016.

3. Wini Warren. *Black Women Scientists in the United States.* Bloomington: Indiana UP, 1999. Print. 74.

4. Danelle Stevens-Watkins, Brea Perry, Erin Pullen, Jennifer Jewell, and Carrie B. Oser. "Examining the Associations of Racism, Sexism, and Stressful Life Events on Psychological Distress among African-American Women." *PMC.* National Center for Biotechnology Information, US National Library of Medicine, 1 Oct. 2015. Web. 15 Sept. 2016.

5. "Human Computers." *NASA Cultural Resources (CRGIS).* National Aeronautics and Space Administration, 3 May 2016. Web. 16 Sept. 2016.

6. Ibid.

7. Ibid.

8. "Stokely Carmichael: Civil Rights Activist (1941–1998)." *Biography.* A&E Television Networks, 2016. Web. 15 Sept. 2016.

SOURCE NOTES
CONTINUED

CHAPTER 6. CHALLENGING THE SPACE RACE

1. "Annie J. Easley Interviewed by Sandra Johnson: Cleveland, Ohio—August 21, 2001." *Johnson Space Center*. National Aeronautics and Space Administration,16 July 2010. Web. 16 Sept. 2016.

2. David Gutman. "WV Native, NASA Mathematician to Receive Presidential Medal of Freedom." *Charleston Gazette-Mail*. Charleston Gazette-Mail, 16 Nov. 2015. Web. 16 Sept. 2016.

3. Beverly E. Golemba. *Human Computers: The Women in Aeronautical Research*. 1995. 43. *NASA Cultural Resources (CRGIS)*. National Aeronautics and Space Administration, 2016. Web. 16 Sept. 2016.

4. "Annie J. Easley Interviewed by Sandra Johnson: Cleveland, Ohio—August 21, 2001." *Johnson Space Center*. National Aeronautics and Space Administration,16 July 2010. Web. 16 Sept. 2016.

5. Ibid.

6. Ibid.

CHAPTER 7. RACE, PLACE, AND OUTER SPACE

1. "Katherine Johnson: National Visionary." *National Visionary Leadership Project*. 2013. Web. 16 Sept. 2016.

2. "Racial Relations." *NASA*. National Aeronautics and Space Administration, n.d. Web. 15 Sept. 2016.

3. "Centaur: America's Workhorse in Space." *NASA*. National Aeronautics and Space Administration, 12 Dec. 2012. Web. 19 Oct. 2016.

4. Gil Scott-Heron. "Whitey on the Moon." *Genius*. Genius Media Group, 2016. Web. 16 Sept. 2016.

5. Ibid.

CHAPTER 8. SCIENCE IN SPACE

1. "April 9, 1959: First Astronauts Introduced." *History*. A&E Television Networks, 2016. Web 16 Sept. 2016.

2. Ibid.

3. "Sally Kristen Ride." *Physics Today*. Feb. 2013. *AIP*. AIP Publishing, 2016. Web. 15. Sept. 2016.

4. "Mae C. Jemison." Biography. A&E Television Networks, 2016. Web. 16 Sept. 2016.

5. "Then and Now: Dr. Mae Jemison." *CNN.com*. Cable News Network, 19 June 2005. Web. 16 Sept. 2016.

6. Cheryl L. Mansfield. "Her Time for Discovery." *NASA*. National Aeronautics and Space Administration, 23 Nov. 2007. Web. 16 Sept. 2016.

7. Betsy Mason. "The Incredible Things NASA Did to Train Apollo Astronauts." *Wired*. Condé Nast, 20 July 2011. Web. 16 Sept. 2016,

CHAPTER 9. HIDDEN NO MORE

1. "Nichelle Nichols: Star Trek Actress and NASA Recruiter." *Makers*. Makers, 2016. Web. 16 Sept. 2016.

2. "Then and Now: Dr. Mae Jemison." *CNN.com*. Cable News Network, 19 June 2005. Web. 16 Sept. 2016.

3. "Nichelle Nichols: Star Trek Actress and NASA Recruiter." *Makers*. Makers, 2016. Web. 16 Sept. 2016.

4. "Star Trek's Nichelle Nichols' Warp-Speed Visit to Dryden." *NASA*. National Aeronautics and Space Administration, 28 July 2013. Web. 16 Sept. 2016.

INDEX

ABOUT THE
AUTHORS

Sue Bradford Edwards is a nonfiction author who lives in Missouri. Her first book with Duchess Harris was *Black Lives Matter* (Abdo Publishing, 2016). She has written eight books for Abdo Publishing, ranging from *Women in Science* and *Women in Sports* to the *Zika Virus* and *Ancient Maya*.

Duchess Harris, JD, PhD, is the granddaughter of Miriam Daniel Mann, a hidden human computer at NASA from 1943 to 1966. Duchess's legal name is Miriam Lynnell Harris. Her mother, Miriam Mann Harris, gave her the family name. Harris is a professor and chair of the American Studies department at Macalester College in Saint Paul, Minnesota. This is her fourth book.